The Angels On My Tree

Written by Lu Ann Schnable Kaldor
Illustrated by Eve S. Gendron

FOUR DIRECTIONS PRESS
RHINEBECK NEW YORK

P
KAL

Published in the United States by Four Directions Press,
P. O. Box 417, Rhinebeck, New York, 12572.

ISBN 978-0-9627659-4-0

LIBRARY OF CONGRESS CONTROL NUMBER 2014953758

Printed in Canada.
Printed on acid free paper.

Published November 2014
FIRST EDITION

www.TheAngelsOnMyTree.com

Because of you and Him.

It was the first Christmas without my father, and my mother knew it was going to be difficult for both of us.

We picked out a tree, put it up, took out the decorations, and stopped.

We stood side by side looking at our tree and cried.

After a while my mother said, "Let's go surround ourselves with beauty; it always makes us feel better."

So we dried our eyes, put on our winter coats, hopped into the car, and headed for New York City.

Snow was gently falling as we approached the Holland Tunnel and when we emerged on the other side it was as if we had entered a Christmas card.

Heading uptown we watched the department store windows pass by, picture-perfect reminders of Christmas past.

We drove along Central Park until we found a spot, parked the car, and headed up the snow-dusted front steps of the Metropolitan Museum of Art.

We paid our admission, pinned on our little badges, took a map, and headed in.

Unsure of where to go first, we let the crowd of people guide us. We wandered and explored, feeling lighter with each step.

As we entered the Medieval Sculpture Hall we were stopped in our tracks by a huge blue spruce covered with life-like silk-robed angels. It took our breath away.

We stood side by side holding hands, afraid to break the magic spell with words.

Finally I asked my mother what she thought all the angels were doing up there in the tree. After a pause she answered, "Thinking of ways to make the miracle of Christmas visible to all."

"Do you think we could do that too?" I asked.

"I know we can," she quickly answered.
"With simple acts of Christmas kindness
we can spend the rest of the holiday season
focused on giving, not getting."

"Can we hang an angel on our tree each time
we perform an act of Christmas kindness?"
I asked.

"What a wonderful idea," she replied.

The ride home was a flurry of excitement as we each came up with acts of Christmas kindness to perform. I wrote our list down on any blank space I could find on our museum map, and when we got home we hung the first angel on our tree.

We spent the weeks before Christmas baking cookies to share with friends, and dropping off casseroles on doorsteps.

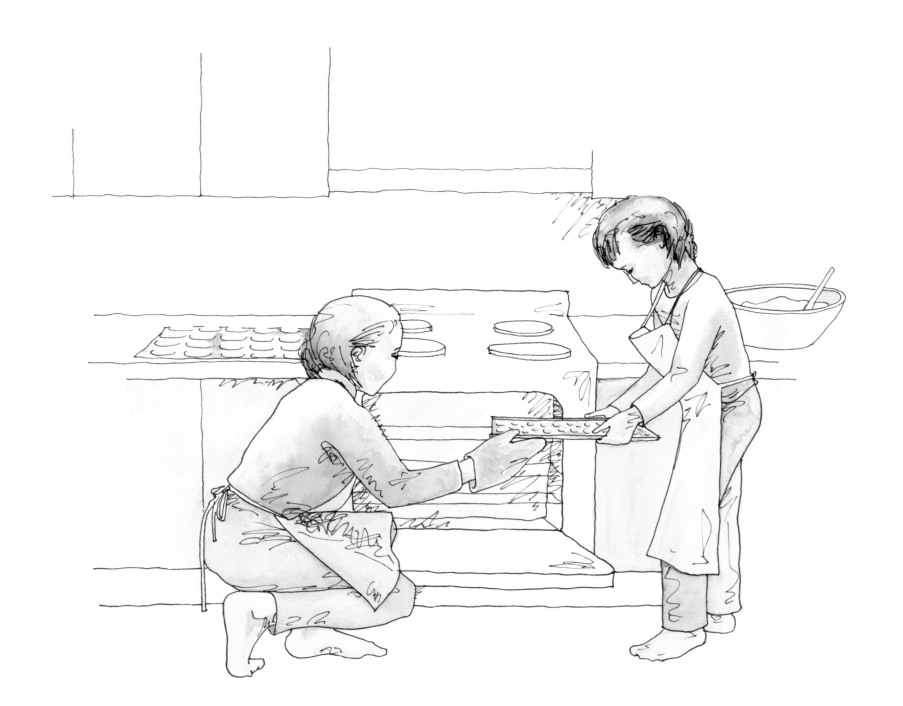

Some acts of Christmas kindness were as small as a kind word...

and others took all day.

We even organized a group of violinists to play Christmas carols at the local nursing home. After each act of Christmas kindness we hung another angel on our tree.

We stood side by side on Christmas Eve looking at
our angel-covered tree, and we knew for the first time,
without doubt, that we were going to be okay.

(Not) **The End** (our beginning)

Thanks, Mom,

Kindness Journal

Kindness Journal

Kindness Journal

Lu Ann Schnable Kaldor
Author

Lu Ann Kaldor is a storyteller, product developer, wife, mother, do-gooder and daughter; a lover of change, sunshine, slow food, classical music, The Hudson River, pinot noir, handmade pottery, NPR, and fried calamari.

After graduating from The Fashion Institute of Technology and Marywood University, she worked in management for Williams-Sonoma and Macy's By Appointment. Lured away by a creative siren, her career included work in the gift industry and teaching third grade. She has put seven stories down on paper, and the first one to be illustrated is *The Angels on My Tree*. She plans on changing the world one little story at a time.

Eve S. Gendron
Illustrator

Eve Gendron is an artist, architect, volunteer, wife, mother, daughter, and Ms. Kaldor's partner in crime. She loves the outdoors, kayaking, theater, cookies, a good laugh, and a great bedtime story. She even started collecting picture books before she had children to read them.

She always wanted to be a children's book illustrator but got sidetracked. With degrees from Princeton University and the University of Pennsylvania, she designed houses, office buildings and schools, but no picture books. Gradually her life included less architecture and more children and laundry. She is delighted to have illustrated *The Angels on My Tree*. The socks remain unsorted.